SNOWFLAKE DESIGNS
Coloring Book

A. G. Smith

DOVER PUBLICATIONS, INC.
Mineola, New York

NOTE

Snowflakes are a perfect example of the wonder of nature—no two are alike! In this book you will find thirty pages filled with fascinating flakes that will provide you hours of coloring fun. You can color the snowflakes with crayon, felt-tip pen, or pencil. Try mixing your color methods for an interesting effect. Color a snowflake in shades of the same hue, or a snowflake in a rainbow of colors to create a piece of art to hang on the wall, or on the refrigerator.

Bibliographical Note

Snowflake Designs Coloring Book is a new work, first published by Dover Publications, Inc., in 2007.

DOVER *Pictorial Archive* SERIES

International Standard Book Number
ISBN-13: 978-0-486-45686-7
ISBN-10: 0-486-45686-2

Manufactured in the United States of America
Dover Publications, Inc., 31 East 2nd Street, Mineola, N.Y. 11501